D1449194

Exploring Citizenship

Sharing

Sue Barraclough

Heinemann Library,
Chicago, IL

www.heinemannraintree.com
Visit our website to find out more information about Heinemann-Raintree books.

To order:
☎ Phone 888-454-2279
🖥 Visit www.heinemannraintree.com to browse our catalog and order online.

©2010 Heinemann Library
an imprint of Capstone Global Library, LLC
Chicago, Illinois

All rights reserved. No part of this publication may be reproduced or transmitted in any form or by any means, electronic or mechanical, including photocopying, recording, taping, or any information storage and retrieval system, without permission in writing from the publisher.

Edited by Rebecca Rissman and Catherine Veitch
Designed by Ryan Frieson and Betsy Wernert
Picture research by Elizabeth Alexander and Rebecca Sodergren
Production by Duncan Gilbert
Originated by Heinemann Library
Printed in China by South China Printing Company Ltd

Library of Congress Cataloging-in-Publication Data
Barraclough, Sue.
  Sharing / Sue Barraclough.
    p. cm. -- (Exploring citizenship)
  Includes bibliographical references and index.
  ISBN 978-1-4329-3312-8 (hc) -- ISBN 978-1-4329-3320-3 (pb) 1. Sharing. I. Title.
  BF575.S48B37 2008
  177'.7--dc22
                                    2008055300

Acknowledgments

We would like to thank the following for permission to reproduce photographs: Alamy **pp. 8** (© Kuttig-People), **25** (© NewStock), **20** (© Ian Shaw), **11** (© Brownstock Inc), **19** (© Sally & Richard Greenhill), **23** (© Big Cheese Photo LLC), **27** (© Greg Wright); Corbis **pp. 4** (© Ken Seet), **5** (© Fancy/Veer), **10** (© Jose Luis Pelaez Inc/Blend Images), 12 (© Ken Seet), 15 (© Birgid Allig/zefa), **22** (© SW Productions/Brand X), **29** (© Emma Rian/zefa); Getty Images **pp. 6** (Manfred Rutz/Taxi), **7** (Clive Brunskill), **9** (Erin Patrice O'Brien/Taxi), **24** (Paula Bronstein), **21** (Lauren Burke/Taxi), **18** (Allison Michael Orenstein/Digital Vision); Photolibrary **pp. 14** (Alan Levenson/AGE Fotostock), **26** (Jupiterimages/Comstock); Shutterstock **p. 16** (© Monkey Business Images).

Cover photograph of a group of girls reading a library book reproduced with permission of Getty Images (Dave & Les Jacobs/Blend Images).

The publishers would like to thank Yael Biederman for her help in the preparation of this book.

Every effort has been made to contact copyright holders of any material reproduced in this book. Any omissions will be rectified in subsequent printings if notice is given to the publisher.

All the Internet addresses (URLs) given in this book were valid at the time of going to press. However, due to the dynamic nature of the Internet, some addresses may have changed, or sites may have changed or ceased to exist since publication. While the author and publisher regret any inconvenience this may cause readers, no responsibility for any such changes can be accepted by either the author or the publisher.

Contents

Some words are shown in bold, **like this**. You can find out what they mean by looking in the glossary.

What Is Citizenship?

Citizenship is about being a member of a group such as a family, a school, or a country. A citizen has **rights** and **responsibilities**. Having rights means there are certain ways that other people should treat you.

Sharing is an important part of being a family.

Having responsibilities means you should act or behave in a certain way. The way you behave affects other people. At home and in school you have rights and responsibilities.

The way you behave in school affects your classmates.

What Is Sharing?

Sharing with friends can be fun.

Sharing is giving other people a piece or a part of something. Sharing is also using something at the same time as someone else. We share many things with our friends and family, such as food and drinks, toys, and transportation.

It makes sense
to wait so that
everyone can
have a turn.

Sharing can also be about taking turns.
Sometimes only one person at a time can
use or do something. You need to figure out
how to take turns to handle things fairly.

Sharing Your World

When you go to the movie theater, you are sharing the movie with many other people.

Sharing is something you do all the time. You live in a home that you share with other people. Your home is part of a **neighborhood** that you share with many other people.

You spend a lot of time in places that you share with other people. It is important to learn how to share and take turns in school. Learning to share is an important **social skill**. It is a good way to make friends.

It is **polite** to wait your turn when sharing things.

Sharing Things

Sometimes you share things because there is not enough for everyone to have their own. You may have to share books or **equipment**, such as a computer, at school. You may have to share toys and games at home with a brother or sister.

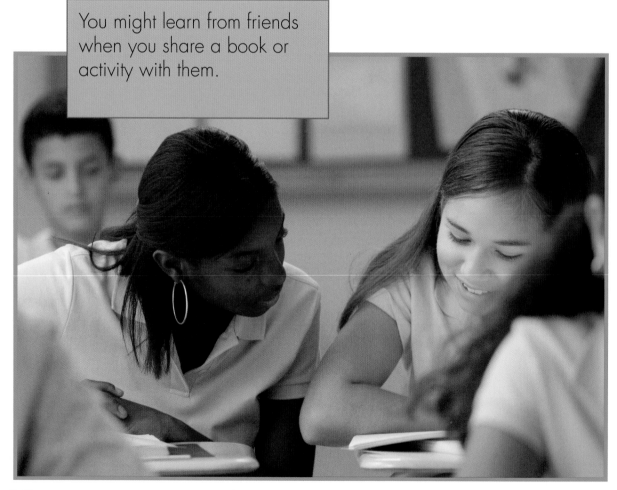

You might learn from friends when you share a book or activity with them.

A bicycle helmet keeps you safe. It should not be shared.

Sometimes it is important to have things that are used only by you. For example, safety helmets or knee pads should not be shared. Other things may be special, and you might want to keep them somewhere safe.

It's Mine!

Sometimes people do not want to share, and it is important to **respect** that. You should try not to get angry or grab their things. If someone does not want to share, swap something of yours.

Do you have things that you do not like to share?

It is okay to have some things that you do not share. If something is especially important to you, you may not trust other people to take good care of it.

If you do not want to share:

☑ do not shout or hit

☑ try to talk about it

☑ explain why you do not want to share

Think about it

If someone does not want to share, try offering to swap something of yours that is important to you.

Showing You Care

If you do not share or take turns, it can make other people feel unhappy or angry. Sharing is not always easy, but it is a friendly thing to do.

When you are enjoying something, it can be hard to remember to share.

Sharing makes you feel good.

Sharing and taking turns can make everybody happy. When you share things with your friends, then your friends will want to share with you.

Sharing Friends

It is good to share friends with each other.

Everyone likes to feel part of a group and to have friends. Sharing helps to make sure that everyone feels that they are part of a group.

How to include everyone

☑ When you pick teams, do not just choose the good players first.

☑ If people look shy about joining in, **encourage** them to take part.

☑ If you have a best friend, he or she can still be friends with other people, and so can you.

☑ Think about how people might feel if they cannot join in.

Think about it

How do you feel when you are left out?

Sharing Space

You may have to share a bedroom with your brother or sister. Part of sharing is understanding that people like different things. It is important to **respect** other people's **property** and their likes and dislikes.

Do you think you are good at sharing things?

You have to share space in the classroom and the playground at school. Learning to join in, share, and take turns makes school a happier place. It is also a good way to make new friends.

In a busy playground, learning to share space is important.

Working Together

Your classmates might be able to help you find the answers when you work as a team.

Sometimes it is useful to work as a team. It is important to learn how to share ideas and work together. Sharing and discussing ideas is a good way to solve problems.

At other times you need to work on your own. Sometimes you need to show that you can do something without help. It is fun to work alone and think of your own ideas.

When you work alone, you have the chance to think about your own ideas.

Give and Take

A good team gives everyone a chance to join in.

Sharing is about taking turns to speak and explain what you think. Sharing is also about taking turns to listen and understand.

It is also important that your teacher listens to you.

You have a **right** to speak and you also have a **responsibility** to listen. You can learn a lot when you listen. Sharing is thinking about what other people might be feeling or wanting.

Sharing Knowledge

Teachers and other adults share their **knowledge** with you. You can take part by listening and asking questions.

When you are at school, everybody has the chance to share their thoughts and ideas.

Is there anything you could teach or share with other people?

You can share your knowledge, too. When you know how to do something, you can share your knowledge with your friends and family. Everyone has something interesting that they can share with other people.

Sharing and Giving

What does your school do to help others?

Sharing is also about giving to others who have less than you. Sharing is about giving away toys, clothes, or food for **charity**.

Sharing is understanding that other people might need help. You can take part by finding out what you can do about it, and then figuring out the best way to help.

You might be able to share money, time, or ideas to help other people.

Sharing and Happiness

Sharing with others is important for happy **relationships**. It makes other people happy when you share your time and things with them. It also feels good to share with others.

Sharing is:

- ☑ being fair
- ☑ using things together
- ☑ taking turns
- ☑ speaking and listening
- ☑ caring for and helping others

Sharing a meal can be fun.

It is important to practice sharing at home so you will be good at sharing at school and in your **neighborhood**. We all share the world we live in, so sharing is an important **skill** for all of us.

Glossary

charity group that sets up ways of giving money, food, or help to people who need it

encourage act or behave in a way that helps someone do something

equipment tool or object that you use to do something

knowledge understanding and facts

neighborhood area around a person's home, and the people who live in that area

polite person with good manners. A polite person shows respect to other people.

property belongings

relationship way in which people feel and behave toward each other

respect way of treating someone or something with kindness and politeness

responsibility something that it is your job to do as a good and useful member of a group

right how you should be treated by others, in a way that is thought to be good or fair by most people

skill being good at something

social skill being able to get along well with others